Jesus

MW01493735

Devotional Journal with Essential Oil Recipes

Visit our website:

WWW.SIMPLYREENI.COM

And find us on Instagram:

@SIMPLY_REENI

WE LOVE CONNECTING WITH YOU!

Today's Oil Blend

YOU CAN DO IT

2 drops Peppermint + 2 drops Wild Orange + 2 drops Lemon

Today's Verse:

TRULY HE IS MY ROCK
AND MY SALVATION;
HE IS MY FORTRESS, I
WILL NEVER BE SHAKEN.
~ PSALMS 62:2

Remember...

I'm grateful for...

Top 3 goals today...

"LORD, LET YOUR WILL BE DONE IN ME TODAY."

Today's Oil Blend

SIMPLY SERENE

2 drops Cedarwood + 2 drops Vetiver + 2 drops Lavender

Today's Verse:

"MY GRACE IS
SUFFICIENT FOR YOU,
FOR MY POWER IS MADE
PERFECT IN WEAKNESS."
~ 2 CORINTHIANS 12:9

Remember...

I'm grateful for...

Top 3 goals today...

"LORD, LET ME REST IN YOUR GRACE."

Today's Oil Blend

DATE:

BE STILL
2 drops Lavender + 2 drops Frankincense + 2 drops Ylang Ylang

Today's Verse:

"BE STILL AND KNOW
THAT I AM GOD."
~ PSALMS 46:10

Remember...

I'm grateful for...

Top 3 goals today...

"LORD, HELP ME TO BE STILL AND TRUST IN YOU."

Today's Oil Blend

DATE:

YOU ARE ENOUGH

2 drops Ylang Ylang + 2 drops Clary Sage + 2 drops Jasmine

Today's Verse:

"BUT BECAUSE OF HIS GREAT LOVE FOR US, GOD, WHO IS RICH IN MERCY, MADE US ALIVE WITH CHRIST EVEN WHEN WE WERE DEAD IN TRANSGRESSIONS- IT IS BY GRACE YOU HAVE BEEN SAVED."

~ EPHESIANS 2:4-5

Remember...

I'm grateful for...

Top 3 goals today...

"LORD, THANK YOU FOR LOVING ME."

Today's Oil Blend

DATE:

GRATITUDE

2 drops Frankincense + 2 drops Bergamot + 2 drops Geranium

Today's Verse:

"LET THE PEACE OF
CHRIST RULE IN YOUR
HEARTS, SINCE AS
MEMBERS OF ONE BODY
YOU WERE CALLED TO
PEACE."
~ COLOSSIANS 3:15

Remember...

I'm grateful for...

Top 3 goals today...

"LORD, THANK YOU FOR EVERYTHING YOU HAVE DONE IN MY LIFE.

Today's Oil Blend

INSPIRATION

2 drops Grapefruit + 1 drop Orange + 1 drop Bergamot + 1 drop Peppermint

Today's Verse:

"BE STRONG AND
COURAGEOUS. DO NOT BE
AFRAID OR TERRIFIED
BECAUSE OF THEM, FOR THE
LORD YOUR GOD GOES WITH
YOU; HE WILL NEVER LEAVE
YOU NOR FORSAKE YOU."
~ DEUTERONOMY 31:6

Remember...

I'm grateful for...

Top 3 goals today...

"LORD, HELP ME TO BE STRONG AND COURAGEOUS."

Today's Oil Blend

DATE:

PATIENCE
2 drops Orange + 2 drops Frankincense + 2 drops Marjoram

Today's Verse:

"BE JOYFUL IN HOPE,
PATIENT IN AFFLICTION,
FAITHFUL IN PRAYER."
~ ROMANS 12:12

Remember...

I'm grateful for...

Top 3 goals today...

"LORD, HELP ME TO BE PATIENT AND KNOW THAT YOU WORK FOR THE GOOD OF THOSE WHO LOVE YOU."

Today's Oil Blend

DATE:

TRUST
2 drops Marjoram + 2 drops Lavender + 2 drops Rose

Today's Verse:

"FOR I KNOW THE PLANS
I HAVE FOR YOU,"
DECLARES THE LORD,
PLANS TO PROSPER YOU
AND NOT TO HARM YOU,
PLANS TO GIVE YOU
HOPE AND A FUTURE.
~ JEREMIAH 29:11

Remember...

I'm grateful for...

Top 3 goals today...

"LORD, HELP ME TO TRUST YOU IN ALL I DO."

Today's Oil Blend

STRENGTH
2 drops Orange + 2 drops Cassia + 2 drops Cedarwood

Today's Verse:

"SO DO NOT FEAR, FOR I AM
WITH YOU; DO NOT BE
DISMAYED, FOR I AM YOUR
GOD. I WILL STRENGTHEN
YOU AND HELP YOU; I WILL
UPHOLD YOU WITH MY
RIGHTEOUS RIGHT HAND."
~ ISAIAH 41:10

Remember...

I'm grateful for...

Top 3 goals today...

"LORD, BE MY SOURCE OF STRENGTH."

Today's Oil Blend

Energized

2 drops Lemon + 2 drops Peppermint + 2 drops Tangerine

Today's Verse:

"LET US RUN WITH
PERSEVERANCE THE
RACE MARKED OUT
FOR US."
~ HEBREWS 12:1

Remember...

I'm grateful for...

Top 3 goals today...

"LORD, HELP ME TO DO YOUR WILL TODAY."

Today's Oil Blend

NEW DAY
3 drops Patchouli + 3 drops Orange

Today's Verse:

"BECAUSE OF THE LORD'S GREAT LOVE WE ARE NOT CONSUMED, FOR HIS COMPASSIONS NEVER FAIL. THEY ARE NEW EVERY MORNING; GREAT IS YOUR FAITHFULNESS."
~ LAMENTATIONS 3:22-23

Remember...

I'm grateful for...

Top 3 goals today...

"LORD, THANK YOU FOR THIS DAY YOU HAVE GIVEN."

Today's Oil Blend

DATE:

WONDER

2 drops Bergamot + 2 drops Lime + 2 drops Tangerine

Today's Verse:

"LET ALL THE EARTH FEAR THE LORD; LET ALL THE PEOPLE OF THE WORLD REVERE HIM."

~ PSALM 33:8

Remember...

I'm grateful for...

Top 3 goals today...

"LORD, I AM IN AWE OF YOU."

Today's Oil Blend

INTENTIONAL

3 drops Roman Chamomile + 3 drops Jasmine

Today's Verse:

"AND WE KNOW THAT IN
ALL THINGS GOD WORKS
FOR THE GOOD OF THOSE
WHO LOVE HIM, WHO
HAVE BEEN CALLED
ACCORDING TO HIS
PURPOSE."
~ ROMANS 8:28

Remember...

I'm grateful for...

Top 3 goals today...

"LORD, THANK YOU FOR EVERYTHING YOU DO."

Today's Oil Blend

JOYFUL

2 drops Bergamot + 2 drops Rose + 2 drops Grapefruit

Today's Verse:

"MAY THE GOD OF HOPE FILL YOU WITH ALL JOY AND PEACE AS YOU TRUST IN HIM, SO THAT YOU MAY OVERFLOW WITH HOPE BY THE POWER OF THE HOLY SPIRIT."
~ ROMANS 15:13

Remember...

I'm grateful for...

Top 3 goals today...

"LORD, HELP ME TO BE JOYFUL IN ALL THE SITUATIONS THAT LIFE MAY BRING."

Today's Oil Blend

CREATED IN HIS IMAGE

2 drops White Fir + 2 drops Orange + 2 drops Cassia

Today's Verse:

"SO GOD CREATED MANKIND IN HIS OWN IMAGE, IN THE IMAGE OF GOD HE CREATED THEM; MALE AND FEMALE HE CREATED THEM."

~ GENESIS 1:27

Remember...

I'm grateful for...

Top 3 goals today...

"LORD, HELP ME TO HAVE A HEART LIKE YOURS."

Today's Oil Blend

DATE:

FORGIVENESS
2 drops Juniper Berry + 2 drops Myrrh + 2 drops Thyme

Today's Verse:

"BE KIND AND
COMPASSIONATE TO ONE
ANOTHER, FORGIVING
EACH OTHER, JUST AS IN
CHRIST GOD FORGAVE
YOU."
~ EPHESIANS 4:32

Remember...

I'm grateful for...

Top 3 goals today...

"LORD, HELP ME TO FORGIVE OTHERS LIKE YOU FORGAVE ME."

Today's Oil Blend

FAITH
2 drops Frankincense + 2 drops Myrrh + 2 drops Sandalwood

Today's Verse:

"TRULY I TELL YOU, IF YOU HAVE FAITH AS SMALL AS A MUSTARD SEED, YOU CAN SAY TO THIS MOUNTAIN, MOVE FROM HERE TO THERE, AND IT WILL MOVE. NOTHING WILL BE IMPOSSIBLE FOR YOU."
~ MATTHEW 17:20

Remember...

I'm grateful for...

Top 3 goals today...

"LORD, HELP ME TO HAVE FAITH."

Today's Oil Blend

DATE:

CALLED FOR GREATNESS
3 drops Cinnamon + 3 drops Cassia

Today's Verse:

"TAKE DELIGHT IN THE LORD AND HE WILL GIVE YOU THE DESIRES OF YOUR HEART."
~ PSALM 37:4

Remember...

I'm grateful for...

Top 3 goals today...

"LORD, HELP ME TO DO YOUR WILL."

Today's Oil Blend

CALM

2 drops Vetiver + 2 drops Cedarwood + 2 drops Roman Chamomile

Today's Verse:

"TRUST IN THE LORD WITH
ALL YOUR HEART AND LEAN
NOT ON YOUR OWN
UNDERSTANDING; IN ALL
YOUR WAYS SUBMIT TO
HIM, AND HE WILL MAKE
YOUR PATHS STRAIGHT."
~ PROVERBS 3:5

Remember...

I'm grateful for...

Top 3 goals today...

"LORD, THANK YOU FOR GUIDING ME."

Today's Oil Blend

DATE:

PEACE LIKE A RIVER
2 drops Arborvitae + 2 drops Lavender + 2 drops Cedarwood

Today's Verse:

"I HAVE TOLD YOU THESE THINGS, SO THAT IN ME YOU MAY HAVE PEACE. IN THIS WORLD YOU WILL HAVE TROUBLE. BUT TAKE HEART! I HAVE OVERCOME THE WORLD."
~ JOHN 16:33

Remember...

I'm grateful for...

Top 3 goals today...

"LORD, THANK YOU FOR OVERCOMING THE WORLD FOR ME."

Today's Oil Blend

DATE:

YOU ARE LOVED

2 drops Rose + 2 drops Tangerine + 2 drops Geranium

Today's Verse:

"FOR GOD SO LOVED THE
WORLD THAT HE GAVE HIS
ONE AND ONLY SON, THAT
WHOEVER BELIEVES IN
HIM SHALL NOT PERISH
BUT HAVE ETERNAL LIFE."
~ JOHN 3:16

Remember...

I'm grateful for...

Top 3 goals today...

"LORD, THANK YOU FOR LOVING ME WITH AN UNCONDITIONAL LOVE."

Today's Oil Blend

REFLECTION

2 drops Cypress + 2 drops Lime + 2 drops Frankincense

Today's Verse:

"THE LORD HAS DONE IT
THIS VERY DAY;
LET US REJOICE TODAY AND
BE GLAD."
~ PSALM 118:24

Remember...

I'm grateful for...

Top 3 goals today...

"LORD, THANK YOU FOR NEVER LEAVING ME."

Today's Oil Blend

PURPOSEFUL
3 drops Ginger + 3 drops Cassia

Today's Verse:

"DO NOT CONFORM TO THE PATTERN OF THIS WORLD, BUT BE TRANSFORMED BY THE RENEWING OF YOUR MIND. THEN YOU WILL BE ABLE TO TEST AND APPROVE WHAT GOD'S WILL IS- HIS GOOD, PLEASING, AND PERFECT WILL."
~ ROMANS 12:2

Remember...

I'm grateful for...

Top 3 goals today...

"LORD, HELP ME TO FOCUS ON YOU DAILY."

Today's Oil Blend

DATE:

FEAR NO MORE

2 drops Cedarwood + 2 drops Juniper Berry + 2 drops Vetiver

Today's Verse:

"EVEN THOUGH I WALK THROUGH THE DARKEST VALLEY, I WILL FEAR NO EVIL, FOR YOU ARE WITH ME; YOUR ROD AND YOUR STAFF, THEY COMFORT ME."
~ PSALM 23:4

Remember...

I'm grateful for...

Top 3 goals today...

"LORD, PLEASE HELP ME FEAR NO MORE, AND TRUST YOUR PERFECT WILL FOR MY LIFE."

Today's Oil Blend

GRACE

2 drops Basil + 2 drops Geranium + 2 drops Lavender

Today's Verse:

"FOR IT IS BY GRACE YOU
HAVE BEEN SAVED, THROUGH
FAITH- AND THIS IS NOT
FROM YOURSELVES, IT IS THE
GIFT OF GOD- NOT BY WORKS,
SO THAT NO ONE CAN BOAST."
~ EPHESIANS 2:8-9

Remember...

I'm grateful for...

Top 3 goals today...

"LORD, THANK YOU FOR YOUR GRACE."

Today's Oil Blend

DATE:

SERVING OTHERS

2 drops Cardamom + 2 drops Wild Orange + 2 drops Rosemary

Today's Verse:

"EACH OF YOU SHOULD USE
WHATEVER GIFT YOU HAVE
RECEIVED TO SERVE
OTHERS, AS FAITHFUL
STEWARDS OF GOD'S
GRACE IN ITS VARIOUS
FORMS."
~ 1 PETER 4:10

Remember...

I'm grateful for...

Top 3 goals today...

"LORD, HELP ME TO HAVE A SERVANTS HEART."

Today's Oil Blend

HEART LIKE JESUS
2 drops Frankincense + 2 drops Lime + 2 drops Lemon

Today's Verse:

"MY SON, GIVE ME YOUR
HEART AND LET YOUR
EYES DELIGHT IN MY
WAYS."
~ PROVERBS 23:26

Remember...

I'm grateful for...

Top 3 goals today...

"LORD, MAKE MY HEART LIKE YOURS."

Today's Oil Blend

DATE:

BEAUTY
2 drops Grapefruit + 2 drops Rose + 2 drops Bergamot

Today's Verse:

"YOUR BEAUTY SHOULD NOT
COME FROM OUTWARD
ADORNMENT, SUCH AS
ELABORATE HAIRSTYLES AND
THE WEARING OF GOLD JEWELRY
OR FINE CLOTHES. RATHER, IT
SHOULD BE THAT OF YOUR
INNER SELF, THE UNFADING
BEAUTY OF A GENTLE AND QUIET
SPIRIT, WHICH IS OF GREAT
WORTH IN GOD'S SIGHT."
~ 1 PETER 3:3-4

Remember...

I'm grateful for...

Top 3 goals today...

"LORD, HELP ME TO DEVELOP THE UNFADING
BEAUTY OF A GENTLE AND QUIET SPIRIT."

Today's Oil Blend

DATE:

FRESH FLOWERS
2 drops Geranium + 2 drops Clary Sage + 2 drops Rose

Today's Verse:

"THERE IS A TIME FOR
EVERYTHING, AND A
SEASON FOR EVERY
ACTIVITY UNDER THE
HEAVENS."
~ ECCLESIASTES 3:1

Remember...

I'm grateful for...

Top 3 goals today...

"LORD, THANK YOU FOR EVERYTHING YOU PROVIDE."

Today's Oil Blend

DATE:

New beginnings
2 drops Wintergreen + 3 drops Tangerine

Today's Verse:

"But if we walk in the light, as he is in the light, we have fellowship with one another, and the blood of Jesus, his Son, purifies us from all sin."

~ 1 John 1:7

Remember...

I'm grateful for...

Top 3 goals today...

"Lord, thank you for creating in me a new heart."

Today's Oil Blend

WORTHY
4 drops Bergamot + 2 drops Grapefruit

Today's Verse:

"FOR YOU CREATED MY INMOST
BEING; YOU KNIT ME
TOGETHER IN MY MOTHER'S
WOMB. I PRAISE YOU BECAUSE
I AM FEARFULLY AND
WONDERFULLY MADE; YOUR
WORKS ARE WONDERFUL, I
KNOW THAT FULL WELL."
~ PSALM 139:13-14

Remember...

I'm grateful for...

Top 3 goals today...

"LORD, THANK YOU FOR CREATING ME IN YOUR IMAGE."

Today's Oil Blend

PRAISING MY SAVIOR
3 drops Frankincense + 3 drop Myrrh

Today's Verse:

"THE LORD IS MY ROCK,
MY FORTRESS AND MY
DELIVERER;
MY GOD IS MY ROCK, IN
WHOM I TAKE REFUGE,
MY SHIELD AND THE
HORN OF MY SALVATION,
MY STRONGHOLD."
~ PSALM 18:2

Remember...

I'm grateful for...

Top 3 goals today...

"LORD, I WILL PRAISE YOU FOR WHO YOU ARE."

Today's Oil Blend

DATE:

Enjoy more

2 drops Orange + 2 drops Grapefruit + 2 drops Rose

Today's Verse:

"COME TO ME, ALL YOU WHO
ARE WEARY AND BURDENED,
AND I WILL GIVE YOU REST.
TAKE MY YOKE UPON YOU AND
LEARN FROM ME, FOR I AM
GENTLE AND HUMBLE IN HEART,
AND YOU WILL FIND REST FOR
YOUR SOULS. FOR MY YOKE IS
EASY AND MY BURDEN IS
LIGHT."
~ MATTHEW 11:28-30

Remember...

I'm grateful for...

Top 3 goals today...

"LORD, PLEASE HELP ME TO TRUST IN YOU AND KNOW THAT YOU
ARE GOD."

Today's Oil Blend

DATE:

PASSION
2 drops Cardamom + 2 drops Ginger + 2 drops Sandalwood + 1 drops Jasmine

Today's Verse:

"FOR I AM THE LORD
YOUR GOD
WHO TAKES HOLD OF
YOUR RIGHT HAND
AND SAYS TO YOU, DO
NOT FEAR;
I WILL HELP YOU.
~ ISAIAH 41:13

Remember...

I'm grateful for...

Top 3 goals today...

"LORD, THANK YOU FOR WALKING WITH ME EACH DAY."

Today's Oil Blend

RENEW
2 drops Geranium + 2 drops Clary Sage + 2 drops Lavender

Today's Verse:

"BUT AS FOR ME, I
WATCH IN HOPE FOR
THE LORD,
I WAIT FOR GOD MY
SAVIOR; MY GOD WILL
HEAR ME."
~ MICAH 7:7

Remember...

I'm grateful for...

Top 3 goals today...

"LORD, THANK YOU FOR YOUR MERCIES THAT ARE
NEW EVERY MORNING."

Today's Oil Blend

DATE:

SUNSHINE
2 drops Lemon + 2 drops Melaleuca + 2 drops Lavender

Today's Verse:

"BUT IF WE WALK IN THE LIGHT, AS HE IS IN THE LIGHT, WE HAVE FELLOWSHIP WITH ONE ANOTHER, AND THE BLOOD OF JESUS, HIS SON, PURIFIES US FROM ALL SIN."

~ 1 JOHN 1:7

Remember...

I'm grateful for...

Top 3 goals today...

"LORD, HELP ME BE YOUR LIGHT IN THIS WORLD."

Today's Oil Blend

DATE:

LOVE
2 drops Rose + 2 drops Frankincense + 2 drops Bergamot

Today's Verse:

"LOVE MUST BE SINCERE.
HATE WHAT IS EVIL;
CLING TO WHAT IS GOOD.
BE DEVOTED TO ONE
ANOTHER IN LOVE.
HONOR ONE ANOTHER
ABOVE YOURSELVES."
~ ROMANS 12:9-10

Remember...

I'm grateful for...

Top 3 goals today.

"LORD, HELP ME LOVE WITH AN UNCONDITIONAL LOVE."

Today's Oil Blend

DATE:

LIVING THE WORD
2 drops Lime + 2 drops Vetiver + 2 drops Rosemary

Today's Verse:

"ALL SCRIPTURE IS GOD-
BREATHED AND IS USEFUL
FOR TEACHING, REBUKING,
CORRECTING AND TRAINING
IN RIGHTEOUSNESS, SO THAT
THE SERVANT OF GOD MAY
BE THOROUGHLY EQUIPPED
FOR EVERY GOOD WORK."
~ 2 TIMOTHY 3:16-17

Remember...

I'm grateful for...

Top 3 goals today...

"LORD, HELP EQUIP ME FOR ALL THIS LIFE HAS TO OFFER."

Today's Oil Blend

DATE:

PEACE
3 drops Spikenard + 3 drops Tangerine

Today's Verse:

"AND THE PEACE OF GOD,
WHICH TRANSCENDS ALL
UNDERSTANDING, WILL
GUARD YOUR HEARTS AND
YOUR MINDS IN CHRIST
JESUS."
~ PHILIPPIANS 4:7

Remember...

I'm grateful for...

Top 3 goals today.

"LORD, HELP ME TO FEEL YOUR PEACE TODAY AS I GO ABOUT MY DAY."

Today's Oil Blend

DATE:

GIVING
2 drops Fennel + 2 drops Lemon + 2 drops Grapefruit

Today's Verse:

"GIVE, AND IT WILL BE GIVEN TO YOU. A GOOD MEASURE, PRESSED DOWN, SHAKEN TOGETHER AND RUNNING OVER, WILL BE POURED INTO YOUR LAP. FOR WITH THE MEASURE YOU USE, IT WILL BE MEASURED TO YOU."

~ LUKE 6:38

Remember...

I'm grateful for...

Top 3 goals today...

"LORD, PLACE IN ME A GIVING HEART."

Today's Oil Blend

KINDNESS

2 drops Myrrh+ 2 drops Sandalwood + 2 drops Jasmine

Today's Verse:

"AND GOD RAISED US UP WITH
CHRIST AND SEATED US WITH HIM
IN THE HEAVENLY REALMS IN
CHRIST JESUS, IN ORDER THAT IN
THE COMING AGES HE MIGHT SHOW
THE INCOMPARABLE RICHES OF HIS
GRACE, EXPRESSED IN HIS
KINDNESS TO US IN CHRIST JESUS."
~ EPHESIANS 2:6-7

Remember...

I'm grateful for...

Top 3 goals today.

"LORD, HELP ME TO BE KIND TO OTHERS TODAY."

Today's Oil Blend

DATE:

PRAISE HIM THROUGH THE STORM
2 drops Spearmint + 2 drops Peppermint + 2 drops Lavender

Today's Verse:

"WHEN YOU PASS THROUGH THE WATERS, I WILL BE WITH YOU; AND WHEN YOU PASS THROUGH THE RIVERS, THEY WILL NOT SWEEP OVER YOU. WHEN YOU WALK THROUGH THE FIRE, YOU WILL NOT BE BURNED; THE FLAMES WILL NOT SET YOU ABLAZE."

~ ISAIAH 43:2

Remember...

I'm grateful for...

Top 3 goals today...

"LORD, I WILL PRAISE YOU IN THIS STORM."

Today's Oil Blend

COMPASSION

3 drops Cardamom + 3 drops Rose

Today's Verse:

"THEREFORE, AS GOD'S
CHOSEN PEOPLE, HOLY AND
DEARLY LOVED, CLOTHE
YOURSELVES WITH
COMPASSION, KINDNESS,
HUMILITY, GENTLENESS
AND PATIENCE."
~ COLOSSIANS 3:12

Remember...

I'm grateful for...

Top 3 goals today...

"LORD, GIVE ME COMPASSION, KINDNESS, HUMILITY,
GENTLENESS, AND PATIENCE."

Today's Oil Blend

DATE:

HE IS MY ROCK
3 drops Thyme + 3 drops Rosemary

Today's Verse:

"THE LORD IS MY ROCK,
MY FORTRESS AND MY
DELIVERER; MY GOD IS MY
ROCK, IN WHOM I TAKE
REFUGE, MY SHIELD AND
THE HORN OF MY
SALVATION, MY
STRONGHOLD."
~ PSALM 18:2

Remember...

I'm grateful for...

Top 3 goals today...

"LORD, THANK YOU FOR BEING MY ROCK."

Today's Oil Blend

DATE:

HUMBLE
3 drops Sandalwood + 3 drops Cedarwood

Today's Verse:

"BE COMPLETELY HUMBLE
AND GENTLE; BE PATIENT,
BEARING WITH ONE
ANOTHER IN LOVE."
~ EPHESIANS 4:2

Remember...

I'm grateful for...

Top 3 goals today...

"LORD, HELP ME TO BE PATIENT AND LOVING."

Today's Oil Blend

New Life

3 drops Douglas Fir + 3 drops Tangerine

Today's Verse:

"THEREFORE, IF
ANYONE IS IN CHRIST,
THE NEW CREATION HAS
COME: THE OLD HAS
GONE, THE NEW IS
HERE!"
~ 2 CORINTHIANS 5:17

Remember...

I'm grateful for...

Top 3 goals today...

"LORD, THANK YOU FOR GIVING ME NEW LIFE."

Today's Oil Blend

DATE:

STAYING THE COURSE
2 drops Rosemary + 2 drops Frankincense + 2 drops Peppermint

Today's Verse:

"IN ALL MY PRAYERS FOR ALL OF YOU, I ALWAYS PRAY WITH JOY BECAUSE OF YOUR PARTNERSHIP IN THE GOSPEL FROM THE FIRST DAY UNTIL NOW, BEING CONFIDENT OF THIS, THAT HE WHO BEGAN A GOOD WORK IN YOU WILL CARRY IT ON TO COMPLETION UNTIL THE DAY OF CHRIST JESUS."
~ PHILIPPIANS 1:4-6

Remember...

I'm grateful for...

Top 3 goals today...

"LORD, HELP ME TO STAY THE COURSE."

Today's Oil Blend

DATE:

BEAUTIFUL DAY

2 drops Lemon + 2 drops Lime + 2 drops Lavender

Today's Verse:

"MAY THE GOD OF HOPE FILL YOU WITH ALL JOY AND PEACE AS YOU TRUST IN HIM, SO THAT YOU MAY OVERFLOW WITH HOPE BY THE POWER OF THE HOLY SPIRIT."
~ ROMANS 15:13

Remember...

I'm grateful for...

Top 3 goals today...

"LORD, PLEASE FILL ME WITH JOY AND PEACE AS I TRUST IN YOU."

Today's Oil Blend

AWESTRUCK

2 drops Sandalwood + 2 drops Frankincense + 2 drops Rose

Today's Verse:

"THE WHOLE EARTH IS
FILLED WITH AWE AT YOUR
WONDERS; WHERE
MORNING DAWNS, WHERE
EVENING FADES, YOU CALL
FORTH SONGS OF JOY."
~ PSALM 65:8

Remember...

I'm grateful for...

Top 3 goals today...

"LORD, I AM IN AWE OF YOU."

Today's Oil Blend

DATE:

STILLNESS
3 drops Roman Chamomile + 3 drops Lavender

Today's Verse:

HE SAYS, "BE STILL,
AND KNOW THAT I AM
GOD; I WILL BE
EXALTED AMONG THE
NATIONS, I WILL BE
EXALTED IN THE
EARTH."
~ PSALM 46:10

Remember...

I'm grateful for...

Top 3 goals today...

"LORD, HELP ME TO BE STILL AND KNOW
THAT YOU ARE GOD."

Today's Oil Blend

DATE:

LIVING YOUR PURPOSE

2 drops Spearmint + 2 drops Lemon + 2 drops Lime

Today's Verse:

"BUT I HAVE RAISED YOU UP FOR THIS VERY PURPOSE, THAT I MIGHT SHOW YOU MY POWER AND THAT MY NAME MIGHT BE PROCLAIMED IN ALL THE EARTH."

~ EXODUS 9:16

Remember...

I'm grateful for...

Top 3 goals today...

"LORD, GUIDE ME IN LIVING YOUR PURPOSE FOR MY LIFE."

Today's Oil Blend

COURAGE

3 drops Birch + 3 drops Sandalwood

Today's Verse:

"FOR THE SPIRIT GOD
GAVE US DOES NOT
MAKE US TIMID, BUT
GIVES US POWER, LOVE
AND SELF-DISCIPLINE."
~ 2 TIMOTHY 1:7

Remember...

I'm grateful for...

Top 3 goals today...

"LORD, THANK YOU FOR THE COURAGE I FIND IN YOU."

Today's Oil Blend

DATE:

PROGRESS OVER PERFECTION

2 drops Cypress + 2 drops Bergamot + 2 drops Wild Orange

Today's Verse:

"NOT THAT I HAVE ALREADY OBTAINED ALL THIS, OR HAVE ALREADY ARRIVED AT MY GOAL, BUT I PRESS ON TO TAKE HOLD OF THAT FOR WHICH CHRIST JESUS TOOK HOLD OF ME. BROTHERS AND SISTERS, I DO NOT CONSIDER MYSELF YET TO HAVE TAKEN HOLD OF IT. BUT ONE THING I DO: FORGETTING WHAT IS BEHIND AND STRAINING TOWARD WHAT IS AHEAD, I PRESS ON TOWARD THE GOAL TO WIN THE PRIZE FOR WHICH GOD HAS CALLED ME HEAVENWARD IN CHRIST JESUS."
PHILIPPIANS 3:12-14

Remember...

I'm grateful for...

Top 3 goals today...

"LORD, HELP ME TO FOCUS ON PROGRESS OVER PERFECTION."

Today's Oil Blend

DATE:

INSPIRE
3 drops Lemongrass + 3 drops Cedarwood

Today's Verse:

"TASTE AND SEE THAT
THE LORD IS GOOD;
BLESSED IS THE ONE
WHO TAKES REFUGE IN
HIM."
~ PSALM 34:8

Remember...

I'm grateful for...

Top 3 goals today...

"LORD, THANK YOU FOR YOUR GRACE AND BLESSING IN MY LIFE."

Today's Oil Blend

CONTENTMENT

2 drops Cedarwood + 2 drops Sandalwood + 2 drops Rose

Today's Verse:

"I AM NOT SAYING THIS BECAUSE I AM IN NEED, FOR I HAVE LEARNED TO BE CONTENT WHATEVER THE CIRCUMSTANCES."
~ PHILIPPIANS 4:11

Remember...

I'm grateful for...

Top 3 goals today...

"LORD, HELP ME TO BE CONTENT IN WHATEVER LIFE MAY BRING."

Today's Oil Blend

PUSH FORWARD
2 drops Wild Orange + 2 drops Grapefruit + 2 drops Bergamot

Today's Verse:

"PEACE I LEAVE WITH YOU; MY PEACE I GIVE YOU. I DO NOT GIVE TO YOU AS THE WORLD GIVES. DO NOT LET YOUR HEARTS BE TROUBLED AND DO NOT BE AFRAID."
~ JOHN 14:27

Remember...

I'm grateful for...

Top 3 goals today...

"LORD, HELP ME TO BE JOYFUL AND CONTINUE TO PUSH FORWARD ."

Today's Oil Blend

DATE:

YOU ARE LOVED
3 drops Rose + 3 drops Bergamot

Today's Verse:

"BUT GOD DEMONSTRATES HIS OWN LOVE FOR US IN THIS: WHILE WE WERE STILL SINNERS, CHRIST DIED FOR US."
~ ROMANS 5:8

Remember...

I'm grateful for...

Top 3 goals today...

"LORD, THANK YOU FOR YOUR UNCONDITIONAL LOVE."

Today's Oil Blend   DATE:

LEGACY
2 drops Helichrysum + 2 drops Frankincense + 2 drops Rose

Today's Verse:

"BUT STORE UP FOR
YOURSELVES TREASURES IN
HEAVEN, WHERE MOTHS
AND VERMIN DO NOT
DESTROY, AND WHERE
THIEVES DO NOT BREAK IN
AND STEAL. FOR WHERE
YOUR TREASURE IS, THERE
YOUR HEART WILL BE ALSO."
~ MATTHEW 6:20-21

Remember...

I'm grateful for...

Top 3 goals today...

"LORD, THANK YOU FOR EVERYTHING YOU PROVIDE."

Made in the USA
Lexington, KY
24 February 2019